KU-581-972

Challenging the Citadel
Breaking the hospitals' grip on the NHS

by Dr Howard Stoate MP
and Bryan Jones

FABIAN SOCIETY

UNIVERSITY OF WALES
LIBRARY
SWANSEA

About the authors

Dr Howard Stoate MP has been the Labour Member of Parliament for Dartford since 1997. He is a member of the House of Commons Health Select Committee, Chair of the All Party Parliamentary Group on Primary Care and Public Health and an Officer of the Parliamentary Labour Party Health Committee. He is also a practising GP and a fellow of the Royal College of General Practitioners.

Bryan Jones is researcher to Dr Howard Stoate MP and a Labour Councillor on Dartford Borough Council. He is also a research student at the London School of Economics.

Acknowledgments

We would especially like to thank Novo Nordisk for their generous support.

The Fabian Society

The Fabian Society is Britain's leading left of centre think tank and political society, committed to creating the political ideas and policy debates which can shape the future of progressive politics.

With over 300 Fabian MPs, MEPs, Peers, MSPs and AMs, the Society plays an unparalleled role in linking the ability to influence policy debates at the highest level with vigorous grassroots debate among our growing membership of over 7000 people, 70 local branches meeting regularly throughout Britain and a vibrant Young Fabian section organising its own activities. Fabian publications, events and ideas therefore reach and influence a wider audience than those of any comparable think tank. The Society is unique among think tanks in being a thriving, democratically-constituted membership organisation, affiliated to the Labour Party but organisationally and editorially independent.

For over 120 years Fabians have been central to every important renewal and revision of left of centre thinking. The Fabian commitment to open and participatory debate is as important today as ever before as we explore the ideas, politics and policies which will define the next generation of progressive politics in Britain, Europe and around the world. Find out more at **www.fabians.org.uk**

Fabian Society
11 Dartmouth Street
London SW1H 9BN
www.fabians.org.uk

 Fabian ideas
Editorial Director: Tom Hampson

First published 2006

ISBN 0 7163 0620 4

This pamphlet, like all publications of the Fabian Society, represents not the collective views of the Society but only the views of the author. The responsibility of the Society is limited to approving its publications as worthy of consideration within the Labour movement. This publication may not be reproduced without express permission of the Fabian Society.

British Library Cataloguing in Publication data.
A catalogue record for this book is available from the British Library.

Printed and bound by Bell & Bain, Glasgow

Contents

"Structurally, we're static. We never think of advancing, altering our system. We say we'll do things and we don't."

The Citadel, AJ Cronin, 1937

Introduction
The future of the NHS

Voters must find it confusing to see a Labour government being attacked by David Cameron for 'NHS cuts' and accused of presiding over a funding crisis in the health service. News reports talk of hospital trusts in financial meltdown, yet NHS spending will be £92 billion by 2007/8, almost triple what it was in 1997. What is going on?

Extra money was desperately needed when Labour got into power. But budgets cannot increase annually forever; this year is probably as good as it gets for the NHS. There may be further incremental rises but they will not be on anything like the scale of the recent increases. Next year's Comprehensive Spending Review will place the focus firmly on the results the NHS can get from its current, substantially expanded resources.

In fact, a period of belt-tightening could prove to be exactly what the NHS now needs. The problem with the NHS is that it is far too focused on the hospital as an institution. The new NHS should be about public health and health prevention, and if the dominance of the hospital continues we will find ourselves unable to make substantial improvements in health outcomes, and the NHS will be ill-equipped to cope with the pressures it will face in the 21st century.

After decades of under-funding, policy makers have been focusing on finding ways for the system to absorb the new money. That has made it difficult to achieve these kinds of fundamental shifts to secure the long term success of the NHS. If we do not achieve them now, the danger is that the NHS will fail. An ageing society, rising public expectations and ever faster increases in medical science creates immense pressures. The strong public support which has been a bedrock of the NHS throughout its history may come into question.

So the tighter financial context must now become a catalyst for real change in the NHS. There must be a power shift from hospitals to GPs and Primary Care Trusts.

The trouble with hospitals

Asked to justify the new money spent on the NHS, politicians can point to how waiting times and lengthy waiting lists for hospital treatment have been greatly reduced; that 79,000 more nurses, 27,000 more doctors, including 3,500 more GPs and 9,000 more hospital consultants have been recruited; that many sparkling new hospitals have been built up and down Britain. And that 99 per cent of suspected cancer patients are now seen within 2 weeks of referral[1].

We can be very proud of this investment, but we should not fool ourselves into thinking that these achievements solve the fundamental problems. The extra money, the staff, the buildings, and the extra operations carried out as a result, are only means to an end. Our objective must be to make Britain a healthier nation. There has been progress here too, but it is not enough. Britain's overall health outcomes have improved only marginally and health inequalities remain stubbornly persistent. Changing the health of a nation requires sustained effort over time.

This is the new health consensus: that the NHS has been too much about providing 'illness services' and too little about public health. Prevention must come first: the experts all agree about that. Engaging the public in looking after our own health is the new holy grail. There is clear evidence – it is better for our health, and could save the taxpayer billions of pounds.

The Government has championed this agenda. For the most part, it has got 'the vision thing' spot on. But that is very different from making it happen. Health policy and health debate is, too much of the time, still all about hospitals. If we want to turn this vision into an effective 'next decade' agenda for health care in Britain, then we need to ask some more fundamental questions: 'What are hospitals for – and what role should they play in the 21st century National Health Service?'

Most hospital admissions should be seen, first, as a failure of health policy. The vast majority of patients enter hospitals as a direct consequence of our failure to spot the potential problem early enough, and either to prevent it or to put in place an effective care package that will enable them to stay at home. Every day, thousands of patients get admitted to hospital, not because they are desperately ill or because they need the support that a hospital can provide, but because we have nowhere else to put them. This is not only a catastrophic waste of resources – a bed in a hospital for the night can cost up to two or three times the price of a room in a top London hotel – it also rarely does the patient any favours in terms of their recovery. No-one wants to be hospital after all, and most patients will make a quicker and more complete recovery whilst in the comfort of their own homes, supported by their friends and family, rather than in the alien and uncomfortable environment of a hospital. Most policy makers, commentators and health professionals understand this, and will talk eloquently on occasion about the need to reduce unnecessary acute admissions and to treat more people in community settings, yet progress is painfully slow.

The most important barrier to change may well not be within the health system, but outside it. For forty years, hospitals have been central to the whole way in which we think and talk about health in Britain and the General District Hospital in every town is a source of affection and loyalty. As a result, politicians and civil servants may see that a different pattern of provision would be more effective but conclude that it would be politically impossible to seek to bring it about.

But we do not accept this melancholy conclusion. The case for hospital reform can be made. We believe that it is wrong to imagine that the public is not sophisticated or mature enough to appreciate the need for change, but we need to change the way we talk about health care.

Firstly, we need to try and change the parameters within which health care is debated in Westminster, and refocus them on primary care. The temptation for Ministers to talk about hospital waiting times and waiting lists, and investment in new hospitals, whenever their record is being challenged, rather than primary care expansion, is understandable one, but needs to be avoided.

Secondly, we need to recognise that a compelling public vision of a primary-care led health service has never been presented, certainly not in terms which can be understood by the public as well as by the health professionals involved. The debates have been couched in technocratic terms, which make much more sense to health providers than they do to patients and the general public. The public get involved very late, and tend to latch on to the familiar – the local hospital – and to respond to a feeling that it is 'under threat'.

What is needed is a much clearer and compelling vision of the possible choices on offer. Are the public really wedded to their local hospitals? What patients want more than anything else is a reliable, responsive health service that can be accessed at their convenience as close to home as possible. Shifting care into the community and downsizing the role of the acute hospital is the means by which we will achieve this goal.

Can that vision be sold? We believe that it can – but only if there is a much clearer 'public offer' of the alternatives on offer. 'Save the hospital' may be a compelling slogan for a local newspaper. But perhaps 'a nurse in every school' would make more sense. At present, we barely have one nurse for every ten schools. And yet a shift of this scale is achievable – within current resources – if we take a relatively small proportion of staff out of the hospital sector. Similarly, a 'polyclinic' in the high street – open to the public at weekends and throughout the week – would bring most care closer to home, not further away, while those procedures which must remain in hospitals can be provided more effectively via an integrated regional hospital network.

This is a 'next decade' vision of the future of health services which builds on important advances in the public health agenda over the last decade. But we also need to step back and acknowledge that some of this Government's reforms are going in the opposite direction, and making the achievement of the broader vision more difficult. We want to see a health service which puts primary care first and which reduces the use of hospital care. This is going to be more difficult if we are, simultaneously, creating powerful, autonomous hospitals and giving them incentives, through the new payment by results system, to compete for business and patients.

The Government has tried to bring about more cooperation and integration between primary and secondary health care professionals. It has not worked. The NHS today remains as factionalised as ever. So we propose a truly integrated model of care, where primary and secondary professionals operate together within single, jointly controlled budgets, and set out the international evidence which suggests this is the most effective way to bring about a much greater focus on primary care.

This would mean an end to the Foundation Hospital experiment, because these hospitals have incentives which would stop these goals being achieved. It is also time to end the use of the Private Finance Initiative for future hospital building. This has enabled many of our most run-down hospitals to be replaced. But the terms of PFI, with hospital capacity being paid for over three decades, are too inflexible to be the right way to meet health needs in future.

These may be difficult messages for government, which has invested considerable political capital in these reforms. But the organisational reform issues should be secondary to the goals we are seeking to pursue. And without these, the attractive public health vision which the Government has set out and championed is likely to prove stillborn, or to remain at the margins rather than in the mainstream of the health care system. We are not proposing a 'one size fits all' model – different areas will want to make different choices about health care provision. But what is required nationally is political leadership in championing the vision, setting the framework within which local debates will take place, and the health care environment to make it possible to give primary care the priority which they require. The balance of power will need to shift. But the first step must be to win the argument for what is needed – by beginning a public debate about what the future of health care for 21st century Britain should look like.

1 | What are hospitals for?

The role of hospitals has already changed beyond all recognition since the foundation of the health service. In the early days of the NHS most district hospitals primarily served as recuperation centres. They had plenty of beds but were able to offer most patients little more than bed rest, with occasional monitoring and a limited range of basic drugs. Simple surgical procedures were undertaken, but most of the more complicated cases could only be performed by the handful of university hospitals based in the cities.

Today's modern district hospitals offer a much more sophisticated range of clinical and surgical interventions. Their patients are generally sicker and have more complex needs than those of thirty or forty years ago, and they expect a structured programme of interventions and intensive nursing. Today's hospitals require fewer beds overall – as patients with minor conditions are increasingly treated elsewhere – but need far more specialist staff and equipment, with intensive care and facilities for radiology, endoscopy and surgery. As a result the overall number of acute hospital beds in the UK has fallen from 356 beds (per 100,000) in 1977 to 241 in 1998[2] (see Figure 1).

Patients are also discharged back home or into community settings far earlier after undergoing surgery than they were a generation ago, thanks to the increased use of less invasive procedures such as keyhole surgery and angioplasty, coupled with new anaesthetic methods. And a considerable number of increasingly complicated operations are now being dealt with as day cases; since 1984 in fact there has been a 341 per cent increase in day cases[3]. Consequently the average length of stay in an acute hospital has fallen markedly: Between 1977 and 1996 for example the average length of stay in an acute hospital in the UK halved from just under 10 days to 5 days[4] (see Figure 2).

But although hospitals beds are now being used in a more efficient way than at any point in the past, it is clear that we could make further reductions in overall bed numbers, without compromising the quality of patient care in any way. Audit Commission evidence shows that if you are admitted to hospital on a Thursday you will, on average, spend a day longer in hospital (6.6 days) than if you happen to be admitted on a Sunday (5.7 days)[5]. This is because many hospitals persist in only operating a skeleton service at weekends, primarily geared towards catering for emergencies and critically ill patients. Patients admitted just before the weekend spend therefore more time in hospital than those admitted early in the week when all of the hospital's diagnostic services are up and running. This is not only frustrating for patients and their families but it means that beds are being tied up for longer than they need to be. Given that 80 per cent of patients admitted as emergency cases leave hospital within 15 days[6], delays of even one or two days in getting discharged, represent substantial and entirely unnecessary increases in the stay of most patients and in the overall cost to the NHS. The Audit Commission estimates that the average trust would be able to free up around six or seven beds simply by reducing the average length of stay in each hospital to that of patients admitted on a Monday.

Reducing unnecessary delays and improving bed management efficiency practices is one thing: the payment by results system should provide incentives for more trusts to reduce unnecessary delays in discharging patients. Scaling back the range of activities and bed numbers is quite another matter – here hospitals have incentives which go against the grain of health policy overall.

One in four emergency hospitals admissions currently consist of people with chronic conditions who 'yo-yo' in and out of hospital, three

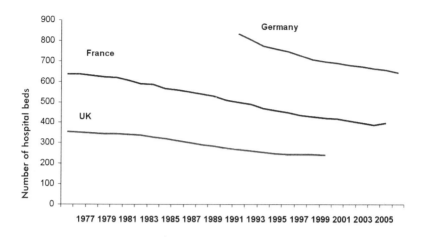

Figure 1 The fall in the number of acute care hospital beds (per 100,000 citizens)

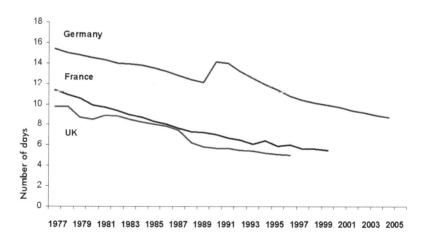

Figure 2 The fall in the average length of stay in acute hospitals

9

or sometimes four times in a single year. This adds up to more than one million unnecessary admissions each year and costs the NHS in excess of £2 billion[7]. We could reduce this significantly by having more staff on hand in the community: This will ensure first of all that patients are better monitored and are more aware of how to manage their condition effectively and, secondly, it will make sure that when a patient's condition does deteriorate that there is a viable alternative in the community to acute admission. But action needs to be taken now if we are to begin to see any benefit from it in the next five to ten years.

Every day thousands of patients arrive in hospital A&E departments, either by Ambulance or under their own steam, with conditions and injuries which could quite easily be dealt with in the community in a primary care setting. Patients are being encouraged to make their local surgery rather than the A&E department their first port of call in the event of a minor accident or illness. More people are visiting their local pharmacist for advice or calling NHS Direct rather than using A&E as the default option. But we are not doing enough. There is now a tendency to label patients as 'inappropriate attenders' – suggesting that it is patients, not the NHS, that are largely to blame for this misuse of A&E resources. That may sometimes be true but can we really blame patients for turning up at A&E with relatively minor conditions, when they find that their surgery has closed for the evening, or haven't been able to register with the local GP of their choice?

What do hospitals need to do?

So making hospitals more efficient will not be enough. We need to stop using them as much as we do. The goal must be to use expensive hospital care only when necessary – and to put more resources into keeping people well, and out of hospital. For this to happen though, we need first of all to end "our obsession with bricks and mortar, as opposed to the actual treatment and service (that hospitals) provide", as the NHS Confederation said recently[8], and to have a far-reaching debate about the role that hospitals should be playing in the 21st century NHS.

The question that we should begin by asking is which services actually *have* to be provided in a local acute general hospital? If we define
our acute hospital as a facility that has the capacity to accept medical
emergencies of any kind, then our starting point has to be an accident
and emergency department, which in most cases will operate on a 24
hour basis. The next question to ask is what facilities and services have
to be on hand to support an A&E department in order to guarantee
safe and effective patient care? An acute medicine unit, in which
acutely ill medical patients are managed following admission, usually
for up to 24 hours, prior either to discharge or transfer to a specialist
care unit is certainly required. A critical care unit for patients requiring
more significant observation or support is also necessary, as is a
Coronary Care Unit. These units will also need to be supported by an
'Essential Services Laboratory' which will provide instant access to
haematology, blood transfusion, biochemistry and microbiology services and infection control services. There will also need to be access on
site to diagnostic radiology services including X-ray, ultrasound and
CT scan facilities.

There are a whole range of acute services that patients need to have
access to, including trauma and orthopaedics, paediatrics, obstetrics
and gynaecology, interventional radiology and emergency surgery,
but there is absolutely no reason why *all* of these specialties have to be
provided at each and every local acute general hospital in a particular
region. This duplication of services is not only very costly, it makes it
more difficult for hospitals to build up certain specialties in which
they have developed a particular expertise. Such duplication can be
avoided, but it does require all hospitals in a region to work together
on a partnership basis as members of an inter-dependent multi-
hospital network of care – each with their own particular area or areas
of specialism – rather than as autonomous institutions in competition
with one another.

This approach would enable us to rationalise the number of specialist beds provided in each local general hospital quite significantly, and save each trust hundreds of thousands if not millions of pounds in the process, without jeopardising patient care in any way. A hospital bed after all does not come cheap: a bed on a specialist ward can easily cost in excess of £500 a night once all the hospitals staffing, equipment and capital overheads have been taken into account. The costs are so great that one leading teaching hospital in London, University College Hospital, has even opted to pay for up to a third of its cancer patients to stay in local hotels overnight rather than keep them in hospital[9]. At £168 a room, a night in the Radisson Edwardian Grafton is not a low-cost option, but as a room on a cancer ward costs between £500 and £600 a night, it still represents quite a saving for the Hospital. And as the Trust itself has admitted, patients who stay in a hotel overnight are happier and more comfortable than they would be staying inside hospital, and as a result make a quicker recovery in most cases.

And then there are the elderly, infirm and chronically ill patients who get admitted into geriatric or general medical wards, with symptoms which could easily be managed in the home or in an intermediate community hospital. Sometimes this is because the support isn't available to keep them at home. In many cases though admissions of this kind take place because the patient or their family are wary about staying at home, and want the 'reassurance' of a hospital bed – even though they probably won't receive much care whilst they are in hospital and will certainly be less comfortable and more vulnerable to new infection than they were at home. Challenging the assumption that elderly and infirm people will somehow always be 'better off' in hospital when they are ill – a notion which surprisingly is still widely held as most GPs will attest – is vital if we are to shift more care into the community and reduce unnecessary admissions. Perhaps the presence of specialist designated geriatric units in acute hospitals is part of the problem. Maybe if these convenient silos for elderly patients didn't exist in acute hospitals; and if we treated all patients on the basis of their condition and not their age; then there would be less temptation to admit elderly patients with non-acute symptoms and more incentive to find them appropriate care packages in the community.

The District Hospital model we have today is largely the product of the early 1960s when Enoch Powell, the then Health Minister, published his 'Hospital Plan for England and Wales'. The Powell plan sought to address the dominance of the large teaching hospitals. The district hospital became the lynchpin of the NHS in each area, providing a comprehensive range of inpatient and outpatient services and emergency cover to a patient population of around 125,000 - 150,000 patients.

This is no longer the right model for a 21st century NHS. But its enduring popularity with the public and politicians alike, as well as with large sections of the medical profession, presents a significant obstacle to change. Politically, this issue has been seen as simply too hot to handle. The umbilical link between a community and its local hospital is such that any elected politician who is not prepared to offer it anything other than his or her wholehearted support is at risk of being summarily ejected from office at the earliest possible opportunity. The cautionary tale of the campaign to save Kidderminster Hospital, which saw the election of the independent MP, Dr Richard Taylor, at the expense of a Labour minister at the 2001 election, has been enough to persuade most senior politicians to keep any reforming ideas they might have private, and well away from the public domain. There seems to be considerably more political capital to be gained from being seen to protect district hospitals, and in reinforcing their rights and freedoms, than in reviewing their role and efficacy in the modern NHS, even if the health evidence points in the opposite direction.

There have been some significant dissenting voices: the Royal College of Surgeons published a new 'organisational framework' in 1997[10], calling for district hospitals to be replaced by a reduced network of larger hospitals, each serving a population of half a million or more. This would allow each region's specialist surgical resources to be concentrated in one place as oppose to being dispersed throughout the area amongst a network of smaller, district hospitals. In the Royal College's view this would enable the introduction of more innovative and efficient working practices than would be possible in a small district hospital, such as the provision of around the clock surgery and diagnostic and imaging services, by capturing economies of scale. Patients would receive a more efficient and technically advanced set of services and there would be more opportunities for professional development of NHS staff. We would not go as far as the College's plan, which proposed dispensing entirely with acute sector provision at district level. An acute unit in each district, capable of providing emergency care for seriously ill or injured patients, prior if necessary to onward referral to a specialist surgical or medical unit will probably always be necessary. There is no single template to which we should be working to: what is appropriate in one region may not be appropriate for others. And it is important that a new system contains a good deal of flexibility and is sensitive to the local health care needs of each area. But we must now start a much more prominent public debate about its merits if we want an NHS which makes the most effective contribution to the nation's health.

Clearly, a strategy for reform must address the question of how to make it politically possible – otherwise we would simply be building castles in the air. But the case for hospital reform has to be made. It is wrong to imagine that the public can not be sophisticated or mature enough to appreciate the need for change. Patients want a reliable, responsive health service that can be accessed at their convenience as close to home as possible. We need to show that downsizing the acute hospital is the way to do that, because it must go together with shifting more care into the community. Neither the politicians or the health professionals have yet made a concerted attempt to put that choice to the public. While patients with acute needs could be referred onto regional specialist centres, most care would move closer to patients, rather than further away: a crucial point in winning public support for a shift of this nature. But we would not propose a 'one size fits all' model.

An increasing role? Why more powerful hospitals won't want to do less

Hospitals, as most GPs will tell you, are foreign countries; they do things very differently there. To the average GP, cost-conscious to the last, a focus on prevention and treating patients closer to home, makes sense from both a financial and a clinical perspective, and he or she needs no second invitation to steer their patients away from hospitals as much as possible. The culture in hospitals though could not be more different: specialists are trained differently and think differently to GPs, and whilst they may acknowledge the merits of a primary care led, prevention orientated model of working, their actions frequently belie this. Hospital specialists still routinely refer patients to one another, without any reference to the patients' GPs, whilst the tendency of hospitals to call patients back for further outpatient consultations repeatedly, even though there is no obvious medical benefit for doing so, is also still prevalent. Encouraging hospitals to do less will require more than just a review of their funding arrangements therefore; it will require a re-examination of the fundamental ethos that governs the working practices of hospitals.

A few acute trusts have begun to re-examine the district general hospital concept and to ask whether it is still capable of meeting the health care needs of the local community. Northumbria Health care NHS Trust, responsible for three district general hospitals and seven community hospitals in Northumbria and North Tyneside, has scaled back its trauma surgery capacity at Hexham General Hospital, referring patients from the Hexham area who need emergency trauma surgery on to other hospitals in the region. The decision has generated some controversy, but the trust has responded by pointing out the limited demand for the emergency trauma surgery facilities and that reducing these activities has given the hospital the opportunity to develop further as a centre for laparoscopic surgery, a field in which it is an acknowledged leader[11].

But we should not get too carried away though by these and similar examples. They demonstrate the limits as well as the scope of what can currently be achieved. The Northumbria trust has not lost out financially as a result of this decision, or necessarily seen any drop in the level of acute activity within the trust. The decision has resulted in a 50 per cent increase in the number of elective procedures carried out at Hexham General, though many of Hexham's trauma patients have been treated in other hospitals operated by the trust. So it is a sound business decision from a financial perspective, well worth local flak that the Trust has had to deal with. While some acute trusts are reviewing the way in which acute care is delivered and operating more innovatively, they are not geared up as organisations to take the next step beyond this, and to work with other providers in order to shift more care into the community and reduce the acute sector workload. Under the current NHS structures, they would be financially penalised for doing so.

Research by the Audit Commission[12] also found that hospital activity amongst foundation trusts increased in 2003/04-2004/05. It found that overall hospital activity increased by around 1 per cent and that short-stay admissions went up by 7 per cent. As the increase was in fact significantly lower in both cases than the overall increase in admissions amongst all acute trusts (5 per cent and 11.5 per cent respectively), the Commission was reluctant to attribute it to the impact of payment by results. The report went on to say however that, "although the picture following the first year of payment by results is that it has had little impact on activity, we can expect to see increases in hospital activity over time due to the incentives inherent in the system". International evidence supports the same conclusion, (as we will see in the next chapter). Another analysis of the impact of the 'payment by results' system, which was introduced for foundation trusts in April 2004, found that it led to an appreciable increase in the number of short-stay admissions to foundation hospitals compared to non-foundation hospitals operating under the old block contract payment system[13]. Between April and September 2004, the number of short-term admissions rose by an average of 24 per cent in the ten foundation trusts included in the analysis, compared to April and September 2003. The average increase in short-stay admissions in the group of non-foundation trusts however was just 17 per cent.

This is a crucial policy dilemma for government. It is rightly championing an attractive vision of a health service which puts public health, prevention and primary care first; a vision that depends on scaling back the use of hospital care, and on using hospitals only when it is necessary to do so. This goal is reflected in January's White Paper, which rightly calls for greater devolution of power and resources into the primary care sector[14]. It also underpins the recent discussions that have been taking place at strategic level within the NHS about the possibility of downgrading the role of certain hospitals – and centralising more care in regional centres – in order to avoid the kind of duplication of services at local level that we have already talked about[15]. Yet, at the same time, government is making the hospital sector, already the most powerful part of the health system, more powerful still. The white paper itself extols the benefits of the 'flexibility and freedoms' that successful trusts have gained by being granted foundation trust status, and makes it clear that the Government has every intention of extending the foundation trust model as widely as possible.

These two aims are incompatible. To put it bluntly, no hospital which is able to control its own destiny, is going to support the removal of a substantial proportion of its beds, even if it can be demonstrated beyond all doubt that it is in the best interests of the patient community. Even when confronted by a reduction of resources, and falling patient numbers, the evidence is that hospitals will try to pursue any other budgetary option, apart from the widescale removal of beds or a rationalisation of its staffing levels or range of specialties. Hospitals occupy a special place in the hearts of the public, and a well orchestrated campaign by a hospital board to resist downsizing or closure can easily garner sufficient public and political support to make any change impossible. Foundation trusts will not sit idly by and watch as the primary sector strips their hospitals of their diagnostic services and specialist clinics.

We have seen this in the reaction of those trusts which have had financial problems this year. Faced with the prospect of cancelled or delayed operations or possible bed closures, even some of the best run Primary Care Trusts have elected to bail hospitals out and make cuts elsewhere, rather than to pull the plug once hospitals exceed their planned activity levels. Those PCTs that have chosen a more hard-nosed approach have often then had to face down a tide of negative publicity in the local media, featuring emotive stories about patients who have had their operations put on hold, and heavy criticism from hospital clinicians.

The Government is now embarking on another round of reform to bolster the primary care sector by restructuring the Primary Care Trusts to ensure they have the managerial strength in terms of financial and commissioning expertise. The aim is to stop them from being given the run-around by better led and more experienced acute trusts, and so enable them to impose financial discipline. Many Primary Care Trusts are too small and inexperienced to manage the resources that they have been handed. But placing more power notionally in the hands of primary care professionals, won't work unless there are also moves to curb the independence of acute sector providers. In fact, the opposite is happening, with the introduction of the NHS tariff system, or 'payment by results', encouraging acute sector providers to try and generate as much business as they can in order to stay healthy financially: the more patients admitted, the more they earn.

This also helps to explain why GPs are ambivalent about the introduction of GP-led commissioning. This should be a reform with enormous potential. In theory, this would give GPs control of the NHS's purse-strings, and allow them to decide which services to commission and where and by whom care should be delivered. Many GPs have welcomed the reform, and have spoken positively about the opportunity it will bring to finally shift NHS resources in favour of the primary care sector. It should enable more specialists to work within a primary care setting and will allow practices to employ more nursing and support staff in order to expand the range of services that they are able to offer in house. But whether it will work in practice is in doubt. After the introduction of the new GP contract, 95 per cent of GPs have opted out of providing out-of-hours care. Many are also likely to contract out the commissioning role to an outside body – possibly from the private sector – seeing it as a distraction from their primary patient care role.

Reforms to the primary and acute sectors can not be undertaken in isolation. As we will see, the evidence from health care reform programmes around the world suggests that change has been slower in health care systems which are composed of powerful, autonomous hospitals that compete with each other for patients[16]. This shows how we can seek to address the tensions within the current NHS reform agenda.

2 | How to put primary care first

Comparative examples and lessons for the UK

Putting more power and resources into primary care, and moving health care closer to home, has been a consistent ambition of this Government since 1997. But bringing this about depends on overcoming the factional divisions which remain entrenched within today's NHS. Efforts to bring about greater cooperation and integration between primary and secondary health care professionals have not yet succeeded, and some key aspects of the Government's reform agenda risk exacerbating these tensions.

The balance between community based health care and hospital provision is an issue for health care systems around the world. The international evidence of where there has been a successful shift to primary care offers some significant signposts as to what needs to happen if we are to achieve this within the NHS.

How to get there: international evidence

In France in the 1990s, a series of regional boards were set up across the country with the aim of cutting acute care bed provision by 4.7 per cent, or 24,000 beds. In five years 17,000 beds were closed. In their place a range of new community based facilities including Alzheimers centres, dialysis units and specialist cancer units were set up. Similarly, in Denmark a decision to put counties – rather than individual hospitals – in charge of deciding what level of acute provision was needed in the area, led to the closure of smaller, less viable hospitals and their replacement by single larger acute centres[17]. By contrast, the Audit Commission found that hospital activity has increased in Australia, Italy, Portugal, Sweden and Norway "as a result of introducing systems like payment by results"[18].

These international examples demonstrate, above all, the importance of ensuring that the strategic responsibility for planning acute sector capacity should not rest principally with hospitals or acute trusts. A planned and coordinated reduction in acute capacity while expanding community based care facilities has been achieved successfully by deliberately choosing to restrict the involvement of individual hospitals in the process. The French example also shows the importance of being as open and upfront as possible with the public from an early stage about the case for reform of the acute sector, and why what it is being proposed will enhance services.

Similar lessons can be drawn from one of the most discussed international health care models: the Kaiser Permanente model of care which operates in California. The Department of Health's White Paper in January cites the Kaiser model as a successful example of integrated, prevention orientated health care and suggests that we could learn a lot from this in the UK. This is undoubtedly true; the Kaiser model has been effective in reducing secondary admissions and keeping hospital stays to a minimum in a wide range of specialties. It owes much of this success to its decision to invest in a network of community based specialty clinics in which primary care professionals work alongside specialists. These clinics have the facilities to cater for more or less every step of the patient's journey, from initial assessment to diagnosis and treatment and eventually to the follow-up appointment. It is an attractive model and the Government is to be applauded for wishing to translate aspects of it to the UK.

There is one crucial aspect of the Kaiser model which perhaps more than any other has underpinned in success in reducing acute sector activity and ensuring that there is genuine integration between the primary and the secondary sector. Unlike the NHS, there are no structural distinctions between the primary and secondary care sectors. Not only is this vertically integrated but its whole care ethos is based around prevention, integrated working and a belief that the best and most cost-effective care that it can give to its patients is that which can be delivered as close to home as possible. The specialist doctors and nurses who work for Kaiser are ones who tend to subscribe to this model and have made a conscious decision to join Kaiser in preference to one of the more conventionally managed hospitals or clinics[19]. It is questionable whether the same benefits can be accrued here if the NHS does not replicate the same level of vertical integration.

We should also look at lessons from one of the less heralded UK reforms of recent years: the creation of single, all-encompassing, Care Trusts through the merger in several parts of the country of PCTs and local authority-run social services for older and disabled people. These trusts were created in an attempt to break down the barriers between the NHS and Social Services, which were preventing older, more vulnerable patients with substantial care needs from receiving the level of care and support that they needed to live independently at home for as long as possible.

Where these trusts have worked well, they have succeeded in preventing many unnecessary hospital admissions, by making sure that vulnerable patients have the right care packages in place in the home. They have been able to minimise the so-called bed blocking which used to cripple the acute system, as the shared care trust budget means that it is now in the financial interest of all staff and managers to keep the hospital stays of patients with long-term care needs as short as possible. Not all care trusts have been able to make the impact that they might have liked. In a number of cases the trusts room for manoeuvre has been restricted by the existence of substantial acute sector debts. But the benefits of having an integrated management structure, co-ordinated working practices and shared financial and service delivery goals however, have clearly helped many care trusts improve the quality of service that they are able to offer patients.

By contrast, the foundation trusts model for acute care risks having a divisive and destabilising effect on the health service, likely to become even more pronounced once the payment by results system is fully up and running. This offers a significant obstacle to the objective of building an integrated, primary care driven health service.

However, the important question is: if you remove foundation trusts and constrain the strategic freedoms of the acute sector, what structure should we put in its place? And how do we ensure that it does not end up merely reintroducing the same problems and structural imbalances that exist now?

Integrating health care in the UK: The case for single care trusts

The need for reform of the way in which acute services are planned and managed is now recognised even within the NHS. In an uncompromising report on the future of the acute hospital the NHS National Leadership Network, a body composed of leading clinicians, academics, and officials, sent out a stark warning about the threat to acute hospitals posed by the switch to tariff-based payment by results, practice based commissioning and the entry in the market of new NHS and independent sector providers[20]. It predicted that many acute hospitals would encounter "substantial turbulence in the years ahead" and in response would choose either to divest themselves of certain services which are uncompetitive, even if it destabilises the local health economy and diminishes patient access to care; or to "soldier on with flagging services" as best they can. The report also suggested as we have that greater integration of care would prove difficult to achieve as a result of the introduction of payments by results and a climate of competition.

In the National Leadership Network's view, the only viable future for acute care, is one that is "firmly rooted in the principles of integration of care and managed clinical networks". Their report was understandably coy as to how this vision might be achieved, or which particular policies or philosophies might have to fall by the wayside in order to allow this to happen, but it did sketch out a picture of what they thought the future care network should look like. In this landscape, the local district hospital would operate as only one component of the local urgent care network and would be "closely integrated with primary care, out of hours care, ambulance care and specialised hospital care". And over time, "key resources," including staff "might increasingly be provided by networks (straddling organisational boundaries), rather than individual hospital trusts".

It is undoubtedly an attractive vision, and one that we wholeheartedly endorse: The question is how do we get there from where we are now? In our view the logical conclusion for the NHS would be to integrate primary and secondary care services to form single discrete trusts. Single care trusts with single budgets have the potential in our view, not just to shatter the divide between the primary and secondary sectors, but to change the way in which health care is delivered in this country.

To be successful this would have to be more than just a re-badging exercise. We can not reduce hospital activity without taking away the acute sector's financial incentives to maximise activity. But this would need to be complemented by introducing integrated care teams in each locality composed of primary care practitioners and specialists with a shared corporate responsibility to treat patients as close to home as possible. Specialists would be based in the community with hospitals providing only those services which primary care practitioners and specialists were unable to perform. All functions except the core tasks associated with short-stay specialist care would be removed from the hospital. The strategic direction for each new care trust would be provided by a powerful professional executive committee composed of both generalists and specialists, charged with ensuring that inappropriate acute admissions are avoided and acute stays kept to a minimum. Financial incentives could be made available to those trusts able to demonstrate the most success in this respect. And in addition to this vertical integration, every effort should be made by these new trusts to establish effective partnerships with neighbouring trusts, so that the vision of managed regional acute networks of care, with each hospital focusing on specific specialties, can become a reality.

The removal of acute trusts would also be a chance to rethink how emergency admissions are handled. The present system puts the acute sector in charge of deciding which A&E patients get admitted, while giving it a clear incentive to admit as many patients as they can under the payment by results system. This makes little financial or clinical sense. The new care trusts would need to take a different approach. Putting a team of specialist GPs in charge of A&E departments would seek to ensure that only patients in need of an acute nursed bed were actually admitted, and also that patients with non-urgent conditions needing follow-up care were treated in the community rather than being invited back for further expensive hospital care. This would also encourage patients with minor conditions to make fuller use of the primary care sector in the future and therefore reduce the number of unnecessary A&E visits over time. GPs have been used in some A&E departments to treat patients with primary care needs and the evidence from this suggests that they been successful in ensuring that these patients are treated more cost-effectively than through the conventional A&E channels[21]. The evidence in favour of giving primary care professionals the chance to take charge of A&E departments therefore is a compelling one in our view, and would certainly justify further examination through pilot programmes.

Ambulance services could operate on similar principles. Patients assessed by ambulance crews as having primary care needs should be referred to their GP, or the primary care out of hours service, rather than automatically being taken on an unnecessary trip to their local A&E department. Paramedics could also conceivably treat patients with more complex needs in the home before referring them to their GPs instead of taking them to A&E for treatment[22]. Extra investment to enable paramedics to improve their patient assessment and management skills would be necessary if they are to triage patients in this way but this merits consideration given its potential to relieve some of the pressure on hard-pressed A&E departments and to prevent unnecessary admissions.

The integrated care model would be an effective way to bring about the power shift within the NHS which the Government's broader vision requires. But it would also suggest not just a reversal of the Foundation Trusts policy, but also a rethinking of current government policy on the hospital PFI programme. Clearly, significant political capital has been invested in the PFI approach. Over fifty PFI hospitals have been opened since 2000, and PFI hospitals now account for around a sixth of the total number of acute hospitals in the UK. Nothing can be done to alter this. And ideological considerations aside; there are no practical reasons why it should not continue to remain an option with regard to the construction or refurbishment of community health facilities, such as surgeries, polyclinics, and intermediate care facilities. Given the state of NHS finances, it might just be the only option we have to deliver the new primary care facilities that we so desperately need.

But the Government could decide that PFI has now served its primary purpose, by allowing the NHS's most rundown and outdated hospitals to be replaced on a significant scale very quickly, within just a few years, and make good on the decades of chronic under investment in NHS infrastructure. Having achieved this, there is now a logical case for drawing a line under the PFI initiative as far as hospitals are concerned, and to look for other more flexible ways of meeting our future acute needs. Continuing to outsource the construction of NHS hospitals to the private sector, and leasing them back on extended 30 year contracts under PFI carries the risk of dramatically reducing the NHS's room for manoeuvre in the next generation when it comes to reassessing acute sector capacity in each area. This could well make the long-term goal of a coordinated reduction in the use of hospital care more difficult. The nightmare scenario is of having to continue to pay large sums of money for hospital facilities and wards that are barely being used. That may not happen, or at least occur in only a few isolated instances, because many PFI hospitals contain fewer, and in some cases substantially fewer beds and less floorspace, than the hospitals that they replaced. But the PFI model is a highly inflexible one which will undoubtedly hamper the ability of the NHS to deliver the objectives of the community services White Paper in moving more care out of hospitals and closer to home. Yet despite dragging its feet earlier this year over the final approval of the long-delayed PFI refurbishment of St Bart's and the Royal London Hospital, the Government's commitment to PFI as a means of delivering new hospitals remains undiminished: Six new PFI hospital schemes, worth a combined £1.5 billion, were unveiled in August alone.

What we are proposing cannot be delivered overnight; and nor would we want to even if it were possible. The NHS is already suffering from a severe bout of reform fatigue, given the avalanche of new initiatives and announcements in recent years, to the extent that it is now with some trepidation that doctors, nurses and managers listen to the news or read their papers in the morning. The last thing we want to do is to add to this fatigue. For this reason we would want the introduction of care trusts to be gradual process, carried out over several years if not longer, after careful consultation with local health professionals, patients and other parties as to how these new trusts should operate in each area.

Patients and professionals would be more inclined however to buy into this reform, if they were convinced that it wasn't just a passing fad, or a policy that could be easily be jettisoned in a few years time, once the political wind has changed. If the public was persuaded that the Government was committed to it come what may, or better still that there was a broad consensus in favour of it stretching across the whole of the political spectrum, then we would have a far easier job of garnering patient and professional support for the idea. So we would hope that the Conservatives, the Liberal Democrats and others, will look seriously at the integrated model that we are proposing, or at least be prepared to enter into a meaningful debate about how an integrated care landscape can be achieved.

3 | Selling the vision
What would a primary care-focused NHS look like?

Even today, nine out of ten patients are treated in the community. But selling any change which shifts care away from hospital beds or services is never going to be straightforward. We all know what hospitals are and understand what they do. Many primary care based services are far more intangible and can be difficult to communicate in a meaningful way to non-specialist audiences.

The failure to communicate effectively with the public has often undermined local reforms in the past: opposition to hospital 'cuts' is relatively easy to foment. But any tendency to avoid public debate on the issue will be counterproductive. The argument can not be avoided; it must be won. Resistance to change can only be countered with a positive argument, and a concerted effort to engage the public with the choices we have over health care. We need to champion this alternative vision of the future of health care in much clearer and more concrete terms than has been the case in the past – turning this into a compelling 'public offer' to bring health care closer to patients. Resources are not infinite. Choices about priorities have to be made. At present, by not making an effective argument for change, the choice is too often framed between a town 'saving the hospital' or losing it. The public can become advocates rather than opponents of change if the alternative to the familiar District General Hospital model is the chance to bring most health care closer to patients, in our schools high streets and homes.

What could a shift in resources make possible?

The model of care which we are proposing would require less staffing of hospitals to free up resources for community based health care. It would be a question of shifting the balance of resources towards the primary sector. At present, these are very heavily skewed towards the acute sector.

Take the example of the number of full-time equivalent nursing staff employed by Dartford, Gravesham and Swanley PCT compared to Dartford and Gravesham NHS Trust.

	Total qualified nursing staff	Acute, Elderly and General	Paediatric Nursing	Maternity Services	Community Services	School Nursing	GP practice nurses
Dartford, Gravesham & Swanley PCT	275	39	4	0	176	4	49
Dartford & Gravesham NHS Trust	611	485	31	93	1	0	0

Table 1   The numbers of full-time nursing staff employed. *Correct as of 30 Sept 2004. Source: Parliamentary answer, 23 Jan 2006.*

Given the current balance of resources (particularly with twelve times as many acute, general and elderly care nurses in the acute sector), it is hardly surprising that GPs find it so difficult to engage in meaningful preventative work or to manage the needs of patients with long-term chronic conditions in the community without having to resort to hospital admission.

Redeploying just ten percent of the general nurses working in the acute trust could dramatically increase the range of activities performed in the community. By having more nurses available to support vulnerable patients in the home for example and more practice nurses to undertake clinics for patients with diabetes, coronary heart disease or

29

respiratory problems including asthma or chronic obstructive pulmonary disease. It would also give practices the opportunity to run more 'well woman' or 'well man' clinics and other such prevention driven, healthy living initiatives.

Looking at the national picture tells a similar story. The Audit Commission study of staffing levels in primary care[23] shows the dearth of nursing resources in primary care, finding that the average number of patients per practice nurse was markedly higher (a range of 3,885-5,202) than the average number of patients per GP (a range of 1,720 to 2,183). Only around half of all practice nurses had the time or opportunity to carry out chronic disease management clinics, which can make a significant contribution to keeping patients out of hospital.

Until we are able to put more nurses and, just as importantly, more health care assistants, into primary care settings, prevention will remain an *ad hoc* activity, undertaken by overstretched staff and reliant on intermittent funding, with wide variations between practices even in the same towns.

The Commission's report found considerable scope in virtually all of the practices surveyed for increasing the numbers of nurse practitioners (registered nurses who diagnose and treat patients) in order to relieve some of the workload on GPs and to expand the range of diagnostic services which a practice is able to perform.

It is clear therefore that in reassessing the way in which hospitals are staffed, and moving more nursing staff into the community, that we could significantly enhance our ability to carry out preventative medicine and give GPs the opportunity to develop their skills further and take on specialist responsibilities. What we are proposing is of course a major undertaking; we cannot expect hospital based staff to move overnight into primary care. Some degree of retraining or at least acclimatisation will need to be made available, and the costs of relocating staff and providing them with accommodation will need to be met. Financial incentives to encourage staff to make the transition voluntarily may also have to be considered as well as guaranteed future career development and training opportunities – although the chance to become more involved in front-line preventative work would be sufficient attraction for many nurses. If undertaken on a gradual basis however, with careful planning, it is achievable, and any short-term cost will be recouped in the long-run as hospital overheads are cut and more patients are managed effectively in the community without the need for acute admission.

Polyclinics

The new model of 'polyclinics' outlined in the White Paper are in many ways the perfect embodiment of the proactive, cost-efficient, integrated, prevention orientated health service which the Government wants to create. In addition to having a significant impact on health outcomes, enabling integrated care and reducing costs, they can also provide concrete examples of government investment in primary care, and so give an institutional focus to the emerging health agenda.

The idea is that the NHS should provide treatment for all but the most seriously ill patients in a primary care facility, close to home. The new clinics won't contain any beds, but they will house a wide range of secondary specialists, such as urologists, gynaecologists and ear, nose and throat specialists and will be capable of undertaking routine day surgery, x-rays and other diagnostic and imaging services. GPs and nurse practitioners will also work in the same building and other professionals such as dentists, opticians, pharmacists and physiotherapists will also be encouraged to set up practice. Polyclinics will operate on a team orientated basis, with teams of GPs, nurses, and one, two or more specialists providing in house care for their patients wherever possible. This creates an environment which allows more co-ordinated, multidisciplinary care involving primary and secondary professionals, to take place.

These may represent a fairly radical departure for UK health care but the concept has been around for almost two hundred years. Polyclinics first emerged in Germany in the early nineteenth century as a means of

31

providing ambulatory care for patients who couldn't afford the price of a hospital bed[24]. They have since had a chequered political history – being banned in Hitler's Germany but becoming widespread in the GDR after the descent of the Iron Curtain, only to fall out of favour again after reunification. Their reintroduction in the last five years as 'medical care cares' (Medizinische Versorgungszentrum), was driven by the German Government's need to control the country's spiralling health care bill: Where it costs around 350 euros to treat someone in hospital in Germany, the equivalent procedure costs just 50 euros when carried out in a polyclinic.[25] It is this capacity to keep costs down that has been at least as much an attraction for UK Ministers as the ability of polyclinics to allow more co-ordinated care to take place.

The concept of a polyclinic is not a familiar one in this country, and so one can hardly be surprised if the promise of a polyclinic in every town has so far failed to quicken the collective pulse of the public and the media. Yet it would be a mistake to let the polyclinic disappear off the political radar entirely, as they have done since the publication of the white paper. They may not have captured the public imagination yet, but once they begin to open their doors to patients this will soon change. It is their sheer convenience that patients will find so compelling: instead of having to travel up to half an hour or an hour to the local district hospital for their blood test, scan or outpatient appointment, most people in any middling town in England will be able to receive all of these services, and more besides, from 'their' local polyclinic down the road. It will bring the NHS as a secondary care provider, back to the high street for the first time in a generation, and provide a highly visible symbol of government investment in the NHS. And by providing a more accessible, less intimidating, one stop service for patients, more people will come forward, and come forward sooner for the treatment or advice that they need – particularly men. So as far as most patients are concerned, polyclinics won't simply just be replacing the services once provided in the local hospital, they will actually represent a significant improvement on what was once on offer to them; and it is in this respect that their power as a political as well as a clinical tool lies.

Promoting health in public services

The nation's health cannot be the exclusive concern of the Department of Health. That has been a core, and welcome, theme of the Government's health agenda. 'Our healthier nation', set the tone back in 1998[26], with its proposal for a 'Contract for health' between the Government, local organisations and individuals, and its focus on improving people's living conditions and life chances, as a means of enhancing health outcomes. It called for a joined up approach across the whole of the public sector and promised that 'action will take place in the settings of schools, workplaces and neighbourhoods'. This theme was developed in the recent public health white paper *Choosing Health: Making healthy choices easier*,[27] which argued that 'Real progress in promoting healthier living depends on effective partnerships across communities, including local government, the NHS, business, advertisers, retailers, the voluntary sector, communities, the media, faith organisations and others'.

Health information has a key role to play. Many patients could have taken steps to help prevent their conditions if they had had better access to good quality information and advice about their health and healthy living. Government has suggested that more information about health and lifestyle choices, as well as advice about housing, employment, benefits and other issues that impinge on people's health, could be made available through a wider range of non-NHS organisations in the community. A more health literate population, comprised of people who are more aware of the consequences of their own lifestyle choices, and are better equipped to manage their conditions and seek the right help when they become ill, is essential if we are to counter-balance the inflationary effect on our health care budget of an ageing society.

The NHS is undoubtedly now more willing to work with other agencies and bodies. There is more recognition among local authorities, education authorities and other public sector bodies of their role in promoting and enabling healthy living. But how can this be made effective? For example, while local authorities are assessed in their Comprehensive Performance Assessment (CPA) on their work to reduce health, relatively few Councillors or senior officers have enough familiarity with the health outcomes of the residents that they serve. How many would include public health on their list of key Council priorities? Similarly, the number of teachers and education officers who take an active interest in promoting healthier living amongst the children in their care is also likely to be fairly limited. The danger is that the topic will receive only cursory attention at inspection time as schools, quite understandably, elect to concentrate their resources on the core curriculum subjects.

In view of this we believe that every school and local authority should be obliged to have its own health champion. At Council level this could be a senior Council officer or an experienced and well-respected Councillor for example. It should however be their principal responsibility, and one that they are able to focus most of their time on, rather than it just being one among a number of portfolios. They should also have a cross-cutting remit, with the license to involve themselves in every aspect of the Council's work, from housing and highways, to planning and environmental health. And every major policy decision taken by the authority should be referred, prior to approval, to them, or a committee chaired by them, to examine whether or not it will help to improve health outcomes, and to see how it can be improved if necessary.

The ideal health champion in schools would be the school nurse. The school nurse should no longer be seen as a peripheral presence in the school, only seen by children when they are receiving their immunisations and vaccinations. School nurses are now expected to perform a key public health role, assessing the health needs of the school community and helping to put in place the strategies required to meet them. They are also expected to get involved in the personal health and social education of children and in the provision of citizenship training. But there are far too few school nurses to fulfil this brief properly, and to influence the lifestyle choices of the children in each school as much as they should. In England 25,300 schools and 8.3 million pupils share just 2,400 school nurses which equates to just 1 nurse for every 10 schools[28]. In some parts of the country though, the situation is even worse. In Kent and Medway for example there were just 49 nurses to cover a school population of over a quarter of a million children in 2004[29]. The Government has promised to increase the number of school nurses. It has made a commitment that, by 2010, there will be 'at least one full-time, year round, qualified school nurse working with each cluster or group of primary schools and the related secondary school, taking account of health needs and school populations'[30]. But this is not enough. Until each and every school has its own designated school nurse, and in the case of the larger secondary schools, at least two nurses, their impact will remain a marginal one because resources will be too stretched to make enough of a difference.

Having a nurse in every school, would give us a unique opportunity to make a decisive difference to the way in which the next generation lives its life; putting in place an essential resource to provide young people with a structured programme of education and support on all the major public health issues facing society today such as sexual health, smoking, alcohol, drugs, diet and exercise. And as well as providing children with more opportunity to learn and ask questions about health in a classroom environment, the presence of a full-time school nurse would enable children to get access to help and advice in private on an informal, drop in basis when they need it most. This could be of particular value for schools in deprived areas with poor health outcomes, whose young people don't always have access within their own immediate social group to the kind of informal advice and support that they need to help them to make informed lifestyle choices. The potential benefits therefore from putting more nurses in schools in terms of improving Britain's health outcomes cannot be underestimated: as

Beverley Malone, the general secretary of the Royal College of Nursing, has said; "this is probably one of the most important things we can do for the health of the nation"[31].

The Government needs to be more ambitious here. This can be achieved, over time, by shifting more nursing staff from the acute sector into the community. That would enable the Government to make good on a commitment to put a nurse in every school without needing the level of extra resources which would be necessary. We believe that seeking to put 'a nurse in every school' would be a very attractive flagship health pledge for the Labour party manifesto at the next election. It would be an exciting development for the NHS which should appeal to voters. And it would mark a clear shift in the focus of health politics from the last three General Elections[32], which have been about waiting lists, new hospitals, doctors and nurses, so sending an important signal about how the Government is seeking to make the case for shifting health care out of hospitals and into the community.

If we are serious about tackling health inequalities in this country then it is policies like this, which will help to give the next generation of young people the skills and the information that they need to live healthily, that we need to pursue.

Since coming to power, the Government has set up a number of programmes, such as Sure Start, designed to improve the level of support and advice about health and healthy living available to the parents of very young children in deprived communities. All this work is of enormous value. But what happens after this once these children enter full-time education and progress through primary and secondary school? In many cases they may go months, if not years, without coming into contact with a primary care professional, or anyone with a public health responsibility. And although their school may try to provide them with some basic knowledge about healthy eating, sex and relationships and so on, it is usually only an occasional, *ad hoc* basis, and rarely consolidated. Meanwhile their middle-class peers are developing, thanks to their families and their immediate social network, the life skills that will ensure that they remain healthy and active well into their old age. That is why school nurses are so important; they are the people who have the experience, the training, and most importantly the time and the opportunity (provided that there is enough of them of course) to ensure that every child has the chance to develop these skills; and so help to break the cycle of health deprivation. They are, we believe, the missing link in our health inequalities strategy.

Getting the vision across

January's health white paper set out the Government's long-awaited manifesto for shifting care from hospitals into the community. Within a week, a storm broke out in the north-west over plans to merge Warrington and Whiston Hospitals. Local politicians lined up to condemn the plan, while the newspapers condemned Cheshire and Merseyside Strategic Health Authority as 'Stalinists'. Even with the ink still drying on the White Paper, Ministers felt they had to rush in to calm the storm, with Health Secretary Patricia Hewitt urging the SHA "to take on board the very real reservations" of local MPs[33].

Once rumours of hospital closures are in the air, the time for debate is over as far as most local politicians are concerned. No MP is going to want to risk being outflanked by their local opposition on so emotive an issue as a possible threat to the local district hospital, and he or she is going to fight tooth and nail to defend their constituents 'right' to attend a local hospital. Ministers too, whatever their long-term policy objectives might be, are always keen to be seen to be putting the interests of local patients before any possible efficiency gains that might be made as result of merging hospitals.

It is vital however that the Government continues to make the case for shifting care into the community. Ministers need to seize every opportunity therefore to underline the Government's long-term commitment to a primary care led NHS, and the critical importance of doing this as far as the nation's health and the health of the NHS's budget are concerned, and to begin a national debate about the NHS we want for the 21st century.

We should be clear too that the role and scale of the hospital sector will have to be reviewed if primary care is to flourish and the sooner the Government accepts this and takes action, the better. If the Government is not honest about this with the public from the start, or prepared to admit that each district hospital may look very different at the end of this process than it does today, then we cannot hope to win the argument and to carry patients, professionals and the media along with us.

We do not underestimate the political challenges involved in making the shift to the NHS we need. The evidence we have so far from public consultation exercises suggest that the public finds this approach to public health attractive. Certainly, most commentators and indeed politicians across the political spectrum know that the arguments for it make sense. But it is not an argument which can be won by publishing occasional speeches and policy papers such as the white paper and hoping that the seed of reform will germinate in the public mind. We will quickly find ourselves once again mired in a cycle whereby the only health stories that get aired in the media are those concerning hospital budgets, waiting times for surgery and hospital closure threats.

This Government has never been reluctant to proselytise, or to pursue a reform agenda, even when it has yet to be convinced that the public is ready to hear what it has to say. But the Government has not made its case for a primary care led NHS in a more a more insistent manner, even though most politicians and most commentators broadly support the strategy.

Changing the way politicians talk about health care can help to lead public debate towards a much greater focus on primary care. There are obvious temptation to champion what the Government has achieved on hospital waiting times and waiting lists. But that will not change the parameters within which health care is debated in Westminster and beyond. The Government needs to remember one of the key campaigning tactics which helped to bring it power and then enabled it to stay there: having identified your message, and boiled it down into an accessible format, you must then repeat it again and again, whatever the circumstances, until it has become ingrained into the public consciousness. It cannot hope to change hearts and minds without a high energy, high profile campaign on these lines. Health ministers, MPs and professionals who believe in championing this agenda need to take every opportunity to put the fundamental case across. We all need to remember, as Bill Clinton might have put it, that 'It's the public health, stupid'.

Concrete ideas to capture the case for primary care – such as the poly-clinic and more nurses in every surgery and every school – can help us to sell the vision of a primary care led health service, with a rationalised and less prominent acute sector. With more nurses in the community and a polyclinic in every town, open to the public throughout the week and at weekends and easily accessible by foot and public transport, we can go some way towards assuaging the understandable concerns of local patients about any possible reduction in the level of acute provi-sion in the area. Far from losing services as a result of these reforms, each community will be actually be able to gain access to a wider range of primary and secondary services, both in the home and in the local community. That is the case which must be made if the public is firstly to understand and ultimately to endorse these changes in the care land-scape. It is a challenging undertaking: but with the long-term financial security of the NHS still very much at stake, the question is, can we really afford not to take it on?

4 | Summary
Policy recommendations for government

- Abandon the foundation trust model and integrate primary and secondary care services to form single care trusts with single budgets to remove the divide between the primary and secondary sectors.

- Put teams of specialist GPs in charge of A&E departments to help ensure that only patients in need of acute nursed beds are admitted, and that patients with non-urgent conditions needing follow-up care are treated in the community.

- Draw a line under the PFI initiative as far as hospitals are concerned, and look for other more flexible ways of financing our future acute sector infrastructure needs.

- Redeploy 10 per cent of nurses working in acute trusts in order to increase the range of preventative and disease management activities undertaken in the community.

- Make extra investment available to enable ambulance para-medic crews to develop their patient assessment and management skills and ensure that patients with primary care needs are referred to their GP, or the primary care out of hours service, rather than being taken automatically on an unnecessary trip to their local A&E department.

- Prioritise the creation of a network of multi-disciplinary poly-clinics across the country.

- Ensure that every local authority appoints its own health champion and give them the power to scrutinise every major policy decision taken by the local authority.

- Ensure that there is a school nurse in each and every primary and secondary school.

References

1   Nigel Griffiths and Peter Murray, '300+ Gains from our Labour Government 2006', Labour/USDAW 2006.

2   European Health for All Database, WHO Regional Office for Europe.

3   'Why we need fewer hospital beds'; The NHS Confederation 2006.

4   European Health for All Database ibid.

5   *Bed management*, Audit Commission, June 2003.

6   Audit Commission ibid.

7   '1 million 'yo-yo' in and out of hospital', BBC News Online, 13 February 2006.

8   NHS Confederation ibid.

9   'Hospital cuts costs by moving cancer patients to hotels', *The Sunday Times*, 20 November 2005.

10   'The provision of emergency surgical services: an organisational framework', The Royal College of Surgeons, 1997.

11   'The end of hospitals as we know them?', BBC News Online 7 August 2005.

12   *Early lessons from payments by result*, Audit Commission, October 2005.

13   Rogers et al, *HRG drift and payment by results*, BMJ 2005, p330.

14   *Our Health, Our Care, Our Say: a new direction for community services*, Department of Heath, January 2006.

15   'Future of ten hospitals in doubt', BBC News Online, 18 August 2006.

16   McKee M & Healy J ed, *Hospitals in a charging Europe* OUP 2002.

17   McKee & Healy ibid.

18   *Early lessons from payment by results*, Audit Commission, October 2005.

19   Shapiro J & Smith S, 'Making the NHS more like Kaiser Permanente', *BMJ* 2003, p327.

20   *Strengthening local services: The future of the acute hospital;*

NHS National Leadership Network: Local Hospitals Project, March 2006.

21   Dale et al, 'Cost effectiveness of treating primary care patients in accident and emergency: a comparison between GPs, SHOs and Registrars', *BMJ* 1996, p312.

22   Robertson-Steel I, 'Reforming Emergency Care: the ambulance impact', *Emergency Medicine Journal*, 2004, p21.

23   *Transforming Primary Care: The Role of PCTs in shaping and supporting general practice*, Audit Commission, March 2004.

24   *The Guardian*, 'Health white paper: The German model: Money-saving and efficient – on weekdays', 31 January 2006.

25   *The Guardian* ibid.

26   *Our healthier nation: a contract for health*, Department of Health, January 1998.

27   *Choosing health: Making healthy choices easier*, Department of Health, November 2004.

28   *Schools and Pupils in England 2005*, DfES/National Statistics.

29   Parliamentary answer, 8 February 2006.

30   *Higher standards, better schools for all: More choice for parents and pupils*, Department of Education and Skills, October 2005.

31   'Call for many more school nurses', BBC News Online, 20 October 2004.

32   Labour's 2005 general election manifesto committed the Government just "to ensure that all school children have access to a school nurse".

33   'Stalinist health chiefs attacked', *Liverpool Daily Post*, 1 February 2006.

Special offer: join the Fabians for just £9.95 and get this book free.

'The Fabians ask the most difficult questions, pushing Labour to make a bold, progressive case on taxation and the abolition of child poverty.' — Polly Toynbee

How can we make poverty history at home?

One in five children still grows up in poverty in Britain. Yet all three political parties now claim to care about 'social justice'. This report sets a litmus test by which Gordon Brown, David Cameron and Menzies Campbell must be judged.

'Narrowing the Gap' is the final report of the Fabian Commission on Life Chances and Child Poverty, chaired by Lord Victor Adebowale.

The Fabian Society is the only think tank with members. Join us and help us put poverty and equality at the centre of the political agenda.

Join Britain's only membership-based think tank

Join the Fabian Society and receive a free copy of 'Narrowing the Gap', worth £9.95, **plus** the Fabian Review equality special issue, **plus** the next two Fabian pamphlets. Call 020 7227 4900 or email info@fabian-society.org.uk for more information.